Marvin Richardson Vincent

Exegisis

Marvin Richardson Vincent

Exegisis

ISBN/EAN: 9783337375195

Printed in Europe, USA, Canada, Australia, Japan

Cover: Foto ©Lupo / pixelio.de

More available books at **www.hansebooks.com**

EXEGESIS

An Address

DELIVERED AT THE OPENING OF THE AUTUMN TERM

OF UNION THEOLOGICAL SEMINARY

SEPTEMBER 24, 1891

BY

MARVIN R. VINCENT, D.D.

PROFESSOR OF SACRED LITERATURE

NEW YORK

CHARLES SCRIBNER'S SONS

1891

J

PREFATORY NOTE.

In preparing this address for publication, I have added a few notes, and have slightly expanded several sections by the insertion of matter (chiefly quotation) which stress of time compelled me to omit in delivery. No essential feature is modified.

M. R. V.

October 8, 1891.

EXEGESIS.

I SHALL speak to-day of Exegesis, its principles, position and function, and its errors and abuses.

What do we mean by Exegesis?

Literally it is *a leading forth, a leading of the way*, as by a guide.* It runs, therefore, easily, into the sense of *explanation* or *interpretation*, by means of which one leads an inquirer to the fact or truth of which he is in search. In the twenty-first of Acts, the word is used of Paul's *narrating* to the elders at Jerusalem what things God had wrought among the Gentiles through his ministry.† John applies it in a somewhat startling way, which, nevertheless, is true to its radical sense, when he says that "the only-begotten Son (or God) who is in the bosom of the Father, hath *given an exegesis* of Him;" ‡ in other words, hath *declared, set forth, interpreted* Him to men, so that they might know the Father. Applied to a collection of documents like the Bible, exegesis is a development and exhibition of their contents and meaning: the explanation of the immediate and primary sense of the writings.

---

* ἐξηγέομαι, " to go first ; " " to lead the way."
† ἐξηγεῖτο καθ' ἐν ἕκαστον, Acts xxi. 19.
‡ ἐκεῖνος ἐξηγήσατο, John i. 18.

In popular phraseology, "exegesis" and "exposition" are used synonymously; but in scholarly usage exegesis is distinguished from exposition as the scholarly and critical from the popular process. Exegesis belongs to the study, exposition to the pulpit or Bible-class. For our present purpose, however, the distinction is not important.

The word "exegesis," etymologically considered, prefers a claim, which it will not be difficult to justify, to the principal function in the study of any religion which is identified with a written revelation. Exegesis *leads*: it *points out*: it *tells the story*: it is the *pilot* and *guide*.

To Theology, therefore, its relation is intimate and vital. In the logical order, in the order of fact, in the order of importance, exegesis precedes Theology. This is the logical consequence of the position of the evangelical church respecting the Bible, namely, that the Bible contains a divine revelation which is man's only infallible rule of faith and practice. For Theology rests upon revelation. Its function is to classify and systematize the material furnished by revelation. Hence its corner-stone must be that form of divine revelation which is most full and explicit; and that form is the written Word. The Bible supplies Theology with its principal materials. Luther indeed was right in saying that "the Word of God is not in the Scriptures *alone*. There was a time when patriarchs and prophets had no Old Testament, and when saints and martyrs had no New Testament." Zwingli was right when he said that "he who is born of the Spirit is no longer *solely* dependent upon a book." Strictly, the

terms "Bible" and "Word of God" are not synonymous.
The latter phrase, though occurring nearly five hundred
times in the Bible, is not once applied to the Scriptures.
As one has truthfully remarked: "The formula of the
Reformation in its best days was not 'Scriptura *est*
Verbum Dei,' but 'Scriptura *complectitur* Verbum Dei.'"
Thus it stands in our own Shorter Catechism.

Nevertheless, though Theology draws upon God's revelation in physical nature and in the human mind, it
interprets their phenomena in the light of Scripture.
They pass through that alembic before they go into the
categories of Theology. As the distinction is really un-
founded between natural and revealed religion, since all
natural religion is revealed, so natural Theology is not,
radically, distinct from Theology as based upon revelation. Nature, apart from God, is a riddle. It is Scripture which brings Nature and God together. Nature
suggests something above and beyond itself; but the
natural man gropes in vain after that something, and
erects altars to the unknown God, until the Word reveals
Him whom he worships not knowing Him. Scripture is
the lens which collects and focalizes the divine rays that
flash from every part of the visible creation. The phenomena of mind, by themselves, provide no sufficient nor
reliable data for a theology. They do not give us God.
Nobody would ever have devised the ontological argument
for the existence of God, if God had not been first revealed in some other way. The word co-ordinates mind
and God. Natural science demonstrates order; but it is
from Scripture that we learn that "order is *Heaven's* first
law."

It is, therefore, I repeat, the function of Theology to take and build with what Scripture gives her. Theology is not a revelation; it is a human structure, built upon the foundation and with the material of a revelation. Its dicta are not final. It systematizes and formulates revealed truth as fast as it is revealed. It throws its details into categories, develops their historical evolution, their relation and coherence, and deduces from them statements of principles and formulas of doctrine.

And this is emphatically true of Theology at its very heart. For a true Theology, like Scripture, is centred in Jesus Christ. He must be the true centre of Theology, because He is the centre and the key of Scripture. Here neither nature nor mind furnish Theology with material. Christ, as a historic personality, is revealed in Scripture alone. Nature provides no Redeemer, suggests none. Christ cannot be evolved by any process of pure reason. The result of Hegel's attempt—"An identity between the known and the knowing"—can hardly be said to be of the nature of a revelation, if revelation means "unveiling." Christ is a unique, historic fact, whose relations to God, and to man's nature, character, and destiny are purely matters of scriptural revelation. If Theology deals with the divine-human personality of the Son of God, with His resurrection, His atonement, His priesthood, His judicial function, and with the work of the Holy Spirit as interpreting Him—it must draw on Scripture. To eliminate the scriptural revelation of Jesus Christ is to wipe out Theology.

Theology, thus primarily dependent on Scripture, is not infallible. Its legitimate *facts* are eternal and im-

mutable. Its *deductions* and *classifications* are not. The
Word is divine and human. Theology is human ; divine
only as it borrows divinity from the Word. Based upon revelation, it is based upon a *progressive* revelation.
Like every other science, it must be a progressive science or forfeit the title. Its deductions and classifications are affected by limitations of biblical knowledge, by
false principles of interpretation, and by faulty exegesis.
Therefore, like every other human product, it requires
revision and correction from time to time. New light is
ever breaking from Scripture ; Theology must have her
windows open and her watchmen upon her walls to discern and proclaim it. The results of progressive exegesis must modify or correct such statements of theology
as are not identified with the *eternal, fundamental* truth
of Scripture.

And thus, however we may, for convenience's sake, draw
the distinctions between exegetical, historical, systematic,
and practical Theology, all theology is, in its last analysis,
biblical. No dogma is authoritative which is not biblical. The first question of Theology is a question of interpretation : WHAT SAITH THE WORD ?

There are questions which properly belong to Theology
rather than to exegesis ; yet some of these questions
Theology cannot answer without the aid of exegesis. If,
for example, a theory of biblical inspiration is to be formulated, that work lies within the province of Theology
and not of exegesis. Yet here Theology is helpless without exegesis. If Scripture anywhere expressly asserts
its own inspiration or defines its character, it is for exegesis to examine that assertion, and to tell us precisely

what it means and how much it covers. Again, a claim
may be made for a particular characteristic of inspiration, the validity of which nothing but exegesis can de-
termine. If it be claimed, for example, that inspiration
involves literal, verbal inerrancy, the claim stands or falls
by the tests of exegesis alone. It cannot be maintained
on the basis of any *a priori* assumption, such as that inspiration *must*, in the nature of the case, mean literal
inerrancy; that God *must* have given His written revelation in inerrant autographs. That is an *opinion* which any-
one has a right to hold, but which no one has a right to lay
down as a dogma or to erect into a test of orthodoxy, until
he can produce the original, literally inerrant autographs.
We are compelled to deal with the Bible as we have it,
and to form our conclusions about it from *what it is*,
and not from any assumption of what it must have been.
Professor Sanday well says : " History is strewn with
warnings as to the mistakes in which we are involved
the moment we begin to lay down what an inspired book
ought to be and what it ought not to be. . . . Is
there any better reason for this than there was for those
other assumptions which Bishop Butler showed to be so
untenable—that a revelation from God must be universal;
that it could not be confined to an obscure and insignifi-
cant people; that a revelation from God must be clear;
that it could not be wrapt up in difficulties of interpretation ; that its evidence must be certain and such as should
leave no room for doubt ? * All these criteria had been
actually put forward; the Christian revelation had been

* Analogy of Religion, Part II., Chap. III.

tried by them and found wanting. No one would think of
putting forward any such criteria now. Yet there is no
essential difference between the claim which was then
made for the revelation itself, and the claim which is still
made for the book in which that revelation is embodied.
. . . It is far better not to ask at all what an inspired
book ought to be, but to content ourselves with the in-
quiry what this book, which comes to us as inspired, in
fact and reality is." *

We must construct our formula of inspiration (if we
deem it wise to attempt that task at all) from an *actual*
and not from an *imaginary* Bible. All that we can do is
to study our Hebrew and Greek Bibles in the best texts
which critical scholarship can give us, and to see for our-

---

* W. Sanday, M.A., D.D., LL.D., Dean Ireland's Professor of
Exegesis ; Fellow of Exeter College Oxford ; Preacher at Whitehall.
"The Oracles of God," 2d edition, pp. 35, 36.

It has been asked : "Why raise this question at all, and so unsettle
the Church's faith in the infallibility of Scripture ? " To this it may be
answered : 1st. That whatever temporary unsettling may result from
such discussion, it cannot be safe to allow any erroneous conception
of Scripture to remain rooted in popular thought. 2d. That the unsettling will be more than compensated by a true and broader conception. 3d. That the question is forced upon biblical apologists by the
assailants of the Bible. 4th. That a defence of the Bible on untenable
grounds is worse than no defence. 5th. That the attempt has been
made to impose the doctrine of the absolute inerrancy of the original
autographs of Scripture as a test of orthodoxy. In the Presbytery of
New York, for several successive years, this test was applied to can-
didates for licensure. The result was to send students to other Presby-
teries or to Congregational associations for examination, and in two
instances men of exceptional promise were lost to the Presbyterian
ministry, and in one instance to the ministry itself, through insistence
upon this unjustifiable and extra-confessional test.

selves whether the contents *are* literally accurate and con-
sistent in date, quotation, and other detail. If, on such
examination, we find errors or discrepancies, exegesis com-
pels us to abandon, not the *fact* of inspiration, but *that
particular theory* of inspiration, and to seek for another
which will agree with the facts.

I shall surely not be understood to say that the presence and the quality of inspiration are to be determined
by critical exegesis alone. Inspiration, however we may
ultimately define it, is the inbreathing of the Spirit of
God into the writers of inspired Scripture; and the same
Spirit acts upon the minds and hearts of the readers.
"The anointing of the Holy One" imparts perception and
recognition of the divine quality of the Word. It goes
without saying that no Christian student can approach
the Scriptures without perceiving that the bush burns with
fire; that no Christian critic can attempt the exegesis of
Scripture without a consciousness of a power, a depth, an
energy, a verisimilitude, a discernment of the thoughts
and intents of the heart, a spiritual elevation and majesty,
which transcend all the results of critical processes and
appeal to something far deeper than the critical faculty.
Yet with the hearty admission of all this, I must affirm
that the validity and inspiration of Scripture cannot be
determined by subjective tests alone. Whatever impression of divine quality the devout student may receive, he
cannot, he must not, in simple loyalty to truth, remit the
exercise of the critical faculty and the diligent use of
critical appliances.

I shall soon have occasion to recur to this point, and
therefore leave it for the present. Having spoken of the

relative position and the function of exegesis, let me now ask you to consider some of its characteristics.

A sound exegesis is *necessary :* it is *critical :* it is *progressive :* it is *courageous :* it is *patient, modest, and candid.*

I.—Exegesis is Necessary.

This proposition applies, not to the Bible only, but to all epoch-making books of remote ages, whether sacred or secular. We all know the necessity in the case of the Greek and Roman classics, and of the earlier English literature. However clear the original sense may have been to the original hearers or readers, the thoughts of men change with the years, and the same thought strikes at a different angle and is reflected from a different surface. Ancient thought does not, at sight, co-ordinate itself with the conclusions, the discoveries, the knowledge, the points of view of a later time. Words do not convey the same meaning as when first uttered. The aroma of an original partly exhales in translation. The setting of phrases is lost, as the customs or incidents which gave them meaning to contemporaries become obsolete or are forgotten. Changes take place even in a living language. The Greek of the New Testament is not the pure Attic of the Periclean age. The entrance of an Oriental influence carries into the language a new imagery and turns its words to new uses. The later Greek is spoken by multitudes of men whose thought is cast in a Semitic mould ; so that, when we read biblical Greek, we need more than the grammar and lexicon which tell us what Greek words meant to Homer or Demosthenes

or Thucydides. We must discover what meaning those
same Greek words carried to a Semitic mind, and how
their meaning was colored by passing into a new moral
and religious atmosphere. The same Greek word would
express quite different moral conceptions to one whose
gods dwelt on Olympus, and to one whose theistic ideas
had been shaped by Moses and the prophets.

Similarly, the proverb is wrought into the popular
speech of every nation, and passes into its current idiom.
The Spanish idiom, for instance, is largely proverbial.
Cervantes's celebrated squire scarcely ever opens his
mouth that a proverb does not drop out. Shakspeare
abounds in them, and Hudibras cannot be understood
without a thorough familiarity with English proverbial
literature. The Bible bristles with them, and they are
often on the lips of the Lord himself. But proverbs turn
on familiar customs, on local usages and peculiarities;
and it is easy to see how the meaning of large portions
of popular speech and literature become obscured with
the lapse of time. The proverb becomes bedded into the
idiom of the language, while that in which it originated
passes away and is forgotten, and so the proverb or the
proverbial idiom is an enigma, until the exegete, by trac-
ing it to its source, restores to it its life.

What is true of proverbs is true of idioms in general. They grow out of customs, traits, habits of thought
which pass away, while the idiom sticks. As might be
supposed, the Bible is full of illustrations of this fact.
Hebrew and Greek are dead languages, and multitudes of
scriptural expressions take their rise in now obsolete and
forgotten customs of vanished races. They are, more-

over, the products of unscientific ages. They are too
narrow for the modern conceptions of the same things.
It is not apparent to the modern reader where they fit
into the wider knowledge and the new mould of thought.
The exegete must discover the old setting. He must ex-
hibit the truth or the fact under the forms in which they
appealed to the hearer or reader of David's or of Paul's
day, and then translate them into familiar forms of speech,
and show how modern science and modern thought correct or supplement them.

The range of exegesis is therefore enormous. It includes the knowledge of many tongues, of a vast range
of history, of a voluminous literature. A book which is
crowded with allusions and expressions shaped by the
history of extinct nations, by the religions and customs
of ancient tribes, by the topography and architecture of
vanished cities, by the local details of countries changed
by years and by successive conquests, by social usages
strange to modern life—a book which, in so many cases
starts from stand-points of thought which have shifted,
sometimes to the very antipodes, with the progress of
knowledge—such a book cannot be made wholly intelligible, cannot be brought to bear with its full practical
power, cannot appeal to the modern mind with its full
vividness, without the aid of the trained exegete.

II.—Exegesis must be Critical.

An eminent and scholarly living divine is quoted in one
of the daily prints as saying: " I see the divine authorship of the Bible as plainly as I see the authorship of

God in the stars ; . . . and when the critics pick
away at the Bible, I say, ' well, it is no great matter : if
it gratifies them, it does not hurt me. As long as all the
universities in the world combined are not able to make
another Bible that shall be so cosmical in its range of appeal, and so mighty in its power over men and women,
over mind and heart and life, and over the growing civil-
ization itself to which it ministers, I rest assured that
this is God's book and not man's.' "

Why not ? Which one of us would hesitate for a moment to indorse that statement so far as it relates to the
power of appeal and to the evidence of divinity residing
in the Bible itself ? No man would feel the truth of that
utterance more keenly, and respond to it more sympa-
thetically, than a devout critic. I apprehend, indeed, that
this writer's sense of the direct appeal of the Bible is in-
tensified by his rich culture and wide biblical study. Why
then that side - cut at the critics, that attitude of benig-
nant tolerance, as though the critic's function were both
superfluous and contemptible ; as though the biblical
critic were a presumptuous intruder into the Holy of
Holies, laying curious and profane hands upon the ark ?
Unfortunately this is a specimen of a large class of utterances from the religious press and from the pulpit, which
go to create the popular impression that the critic is the
enemy of Scripture. Must it indeed be assumed that
the biblical critic is animated mainly or solely by the
love of picking flaws ? Is the critic to be placarded as
an intruder and his function as gratuitously assumed ?
Before I shall have finished, I hope to show, by facts of
the history of exegesis, that the biblical critic has been

made a necessity by the superstition, the ignorance, and
the unhallowed ambition which have applied the wrench
to Scripture, and have wrested it to the service of ecclesi-
astical fraud, spiritual tyranny, and popular amusement.
Ah! the critic's work is not always the work which the
critic himself courts. I have sometimes thought that
there was danger of the Bible being spoiled for some of
us, as Milton's "Paradise Lost" was, by our being forced
to use it for parsing. I heard a veteran biblical critic say,
not three weeks ago: "I wish they would let us preach
the truth there is in the Bible, instead of forcing us to
treat it critically." But the necessity of criticism lies in
the structure of the Bible itself. Its function is construc-
tive no less than destructive. The conception of the
biblical critic as a mere flaw-picker, is a conception born
of ignorance. The devout Christian criticism of the
present century, if it be carefully studied, will be found
(so far as it has been destructive) to have been a picking
of flaws, not in the Bible, but in the monstrosities of interpretation with which men have overlaid it. The critic's
work has been, to an extent appreciated only by scholars,
a clearing away of *débris*. If men, under the power of a
mistaken reverance, have claimed for the Bible what it
does not claim for itself, they have wounded Truth in the
house of her friends ; and the critic is neither unneces-
sary, irreverent, nor contemptible, who, by enabling the
Bible to tell its own story and to voice its own claims,
heals the wound and exposes the clumsiness of the hands
which have dealt it.

I repeat, therefore, that a true exegesis is critical.
Practically, criticism and exegesis are so bound up to-

2

gether that it is impossible to separate them. Exegesis
can advance hardly a step without applying the processes or the results of criticism. Its very first question is
the question of the text, which is a matter belonging to
criticism. The Pauline authorship of the Epistle to the
Hebrews is a question of criticism ; yet the interpretation of a disputed passage in that Epistle may turn upon
whether the passage has a Pauline coloring and is to be
considered from a Pauline standpoint. Baur's theory that
the Gospel of John is a dogmatic tendency-document of
the second century, will require a very different exegesis to
that which starts from the evangelical position. If the
book of Acts is a conciliatory treatise by a Paulinist, written in order to reconcile the opinions of Paul and Peter ;
if the diary of an unknown companion of Paul has been in-
corporated into a fictitious narrative, intended to disguise
the early history of the Church, the splendid exegeses of
Hackett, Meyer, and Gloag are comparatively useless.

By "criticism " I mean the application of the canons of
philology, history, and grammar to the determination and
interpretation of the Scripture text. I mean that the
same laws are to be applied to the Scriptures as to any
other book. The Bible comes to men through the medium of human speech ; its utterances obey the ordinary
laws of language ; its imagery is drawn from the familiar
facts of nature and of human life ; its scientific statements are conditioned by the limitations of human
knowledge at the time they were made ; it is a revelation
given, as the writer to the Hebrews says, "by divers portions and in divers manners ; " * a revelation not made all

* Heb. i. 1: πολυμερῶς καὶ πολυτρόπως.

at once, but by a long and gradual process, and through individuals of different characters, attainments, and temperaments. Inspiration does not obliterate these differences. It does not reduce the style of Scripture to a monotonous uniformity. It does not make of the several writers mere transcribers of a copy or literal reporters of a verbal dictation. Their peculiar characteristics of mind, temperament, and culture are stamped upon their prophecies, gospels, epistles, and narratives. John differs from Paul, Paul from James, and Peter from all three. The medium of the revelation, I repeat, is human. It must be in order to be intelligible. A revelation through an unintelligible medium is a contradiction in terms. The written Word, like the personal Word, is "made flesh." As there is both a divine and a human element in the incarnate Word, so the same elements exist and demand distinct recognition in the written Word. "The law," as Maimonides said, "speaks in the tongues of men." A David or a Sampson may be vehicles of the Spirit of God, yet liable to gross sins. Light is light, though it come to the eye through cracked or colored glass. Similarly, the Spirit may speak through a human writer without eliminating his human characteristics. The imprecatory Psalms speak the language of human passion ; the vehemence of the apostle who cut off Malchus' ear is not absent from his epistles; Paul betrays the influence of his rabbinical training in the discussion of Christian themes. The Spirit utters heavenly truth through illustrations which appeal to human knowledge of every-day facts ; the truth is cast in the mould of one age or another, and takes color from its local and temporary traits, and is expounded according to its literary methods. The transcendent character of Scripture, in short, does not reside in these details.

From all this the inference is inevitable that the revelation in Scripture submits itself to critical tests and invites them; that the human medium is subject to examination according to those literary, grammatical, philological, psychological, and historical laws which we apply to other human productions. In a word, inspiration cannot refuse the tests appropriate to those human media through which it has chosen to transmit itself.

This is not to say that portions of Scripture may not, for the time, transcend the human understanding. Christ did not scruple to say to His disciples things which they did not understand at the moment. Revelation is very often germinal. Exegesis cannot explain everything. But revelation is meant to be, ultimately, *intelligible :* and we are not passively to accept enigmas on the assumption that inspiration is essentially oracular and vague. "It is the spirit that is in man, and the inspiration of the Almighty which giveth him *understanding.*" * Revelation is *unveiling;* and while we must sometimes frankly admit and face the inexplicable, while the veil sometimes resists the human hand, far oftener it yields to the touch of reverent criticism. Beneath her veil Truth beckons; and for criticism to refuse her invitation is as foolish as to refuse to cut the emerald or the diamond because God has enwrapped them with hard crusts.

Equally there is a divine element in Scripture. This will not yield up its full significance to merely critical

* Job xxxii. 8.

tests. Something other and higher than the critical faculty is needed. Christ is the analogue of Scripture—a fact which demands much more attention and emphasis than it has yet received. The disciples who could see His face and touch His hand could not apprehend the mystery of His divine personality; and there was an element in His words which, though felt, eluded their analysis. There is the same combination in the written Word. Therefore, I repeat, the office of the Divine Spirit in interpretation is to be distinctly recognized. It may be positively asserted that the Holy Spirit bestows special illumination and guidance upon the devout reader and student of Scripture. It must be admitted that, in certain cases, the insight thus imparted may be clearer and more direct and truthful than that of the mere critic. Those who are familiar with the great exegetes know what beautiful and fruitful results are evolved when the critical and the spiritual faculties work in concert and at their highest power. A notable illustration is furnished by Bishop Westcott, in his treatment of the writings of John. The secret of his power in unfolding the treasures of the Fourth Gospel lies, not only in his critical insight and rare analytic power, but also in his pervasion with the spirit of John's Master and Lord. It is a writer who is regarded as very far from orthodox who says : "He is to be said to understand a writer who, in reading, thinks the same thing which he thought while he was writing." *

All this is to be not only conceded but urged. I may quote at this point the lucid words of my colleague, Dr.

* Kuenen.

Briggs : " The Scriptures must be interpreted as other human writings, yet their peculiarities and differences from other human writings must be recognized, especially the supreme, determining difference of their inspiration by the Spirit of God, in accordance with which they require not only a sympathy with the human element, in the sound judgment and practical sense of the grammarian, the critical investigation of the historian, and the æsthetic taste of the man of letters, but also a sympathy with the divine element, an inquiring, reverent spirit, to be enlightened by the Spirit of God, without which no exposition of the Scriptures as sacred, inspired writings is possible." *

Yet with all this, I must frankly say that, in my judgment, the " formal principle " of the Reformation needs guarding and qualifying. That principle is that the divine authority of Scripture is self-evidencing, that the regenerate man needs no other evidence, and that only the regenerate can appreciate the evidence. The principle is formulated in the Westminster Confession :† " The authority of Holy Scripture, for which it ought to be believed and obeyed, dependeth not upon the testimony of any man or church, but *wholly* upon God, the author thereof." And again : " The Supreme Judge, by which all controversies of religion are to be determined, and all decrees of councils, opinions of ancient writers, doctrines of men, and private spirits are to be examined, and in whose sentence we are to rest, can be no other but the Holy Spirit speaking in the Scripture."

* Biblical Study, p. 27.
† Chap. I., Sec. 4, Sec. 10.

Now, if that principle is to be nakedly accepted, no other inference seems to me to be possible than that every man is his own judge and interpreter of Scripture; and that, as Dr. Charteris says, "if the regenerate man do not feel the evidence of their contents, he may reject books claiming to be Holy Scripture." It is assuredly true, in one aspect, that the authority and credibility of Scripture depend upon God. Scripture has no authority if it do not derive it from God. But are we to exclude the testimony of man, and of the Church, and of scholarship as going to establish the authority of Scripture? How did we get the Bible at all save through the Church? Who determined the canon of Scripture? On what do the Westminster Confession and the Thirty-nine Articles rest their list of canonical books, but on the testimony of the Fathers and the declarations of Church Councils? Again, if Scripture reveals a divine authority which commends it to the universal acceptance and faith of believers, how does it happen that believers have never wholly agreed as to what is to be received as Holy Scripture? How comes it that Hebrews, the Apocalypse, second Peter, Second and Third John, James, and Jude, were so early and so persistently challenged and placed by high Church authorities among "antilegomena?" How is it that the Apostolic Fathers appeal to the apocryphal writings as of inspired authority, and build arguments upon them? That Irenæus quotes Baruch and Bel and the Dragon as genuine scriptures, and Clement of Alexandria the Revelation of Peter and the Epistle of Barnabas; and that Origen distinguishes Hebrews from books *manifestly* canonical? How came it, moreover, that

the third Council of Carthage, which ratified the New
Testament canon as at present received, under the direct
influence of Augustine, included in its Old Testament
canon, Tobit, Judith, and the two books of Maccabees?
Really these diversities among the early church fathers,
between the Eastern and Western churches, between Carthage and Trent and Westminster, are not easy to explain
on the assumption that the thirty-nine books of the Old
Testament and the twenty-seven books of the New Testament furnish their own convincing demonstration that
they are inspired and canonical.

Now, it is true that the Holy Spirit is promised to believers to give them knowledge of the truth; and that
devout, critical exegesis cannot evade the influence of that
fact, as indeed it has no desire to do. Hence it may be
true that, in certain cases, as has been said, the insight
of a saint may be of more value than the skill of a grammarian. But all this must be offset and guarded by the
distinction between fundamental, saving, practical truth
and matter which, though equally inspired, lies outside
of these categories. The most ignorant Bible - reader,
approaching the Bible in faith, and in search of the
ground of his salvation and the rule of his life, will find
these there. But there are other things in Scripture
concerning which the mere insight of a saint is worth
little or nothing. I do not understand that the Spirit
promises or undertakes to enlighten an unlearned reader
on points of critical scholarship. God does not usually
do for men what they can do for themselves. Only divine
power can change the water into wine, but human hands
can fill the jars with water. "The natural man discerneth

not the things of the Spirit of God;" therefore he needs
supernatural light to dispel the darkness that is in him;
and this the Spirit bestows. But the natural man does
or may know his Hebrew and Greek grammars. He can
discern the force of the aorist tense and of the subjunc-
tive mood. He can weigh the evidence for a reading and
detect and correct a mistranslation: and here the Spirit
throws him upon his lexicon and grammar. The insight
of a saint, apart from scholarly criticism, throws no light
on the genuineness of the passage concerning the three
heavenly witnesses, and of the first eleven verses of the
eighth of John; nor upon the authenticity of the last
twelve verses of Mark's Gospel, of Second Peter, of the
Epistle to the Hebrews; nor upon the meaning of baptism for the dead and the woman having power on her
head because of the angels. Piety and orthodoxy, by
themselves, are helpless in the presence of such questions.
Therefore, whatever may be the self-evidencing authority
of the Bible, it is bound up with intelligent exegesis at
all points which fall within the range of critical scholarship. The doctrine of a spiritual sense in Scripture
which is independent of exegesis has no foundation.
There is no inspired Scripture which will not, ultimately,
tally, in its spiritual sense and in every other sense, with
the results of a sound exegesis.

In short, the principle must be maintained, that the
Bible cannot be correctly and adequately interpreted from
a merely subjective stand-point. Whatever virtue may be
conceded to the subjective insight, there must be objective standards of interpretation. The claim of final authority for subjective interpretation is compelled to face

and to deal as best it can with the endless diversities of
interpretation among men who may be fairly presumed
to be alike sincere, reverent, and moved by the Holy
Spirit. There is but one resource for us, unless we con-
sent to fall back passively upon the principle of the earlier mediæval exegesis, that the Church alone is the infallible interpreter of Scripture—and that is the consensus
of devout and scholarly criticism, combined with the testimony of the Holy Spirit. The promise of the Spirit's
illumination includes the illumination of the critical processes. The Spirit employs all human media. If, in certain cases, He works through the untrained faculty of the
unlearned, He likewise works through the trained intel-
lect, the rich knowledge, and the disciplined acumen of
the scholar. For the docile and honest student of the
Bible, the critical attitude will not impair the simplicity
of heart to which God delights to reveal His truth. It
will enhance that high and reverent esteem for Scripture;
that sense of " the heavenliness of the matter, the efficacy
of the doctrine, the majesty of the style, the full discovery
it makes of the only way of man's salvation, and the many
other incomparable excellencies." All these will come
into clearer light and sharper definition, vindicating the
profitableness of all inspired Scripture "for teaching, for
reproof, for correction, for instruction which is in right-
eousness, that the man of God may be complete, furnished
completely unto every good work."

III.—Exegesis is Progressive.

That exegesis is *progressive* follows from what has been said as to its necessity, and also from the very nature of revelation itself, which is progressive. It has not ceased to be true that God speaks "in many parts and in divers ways." Each part, each way unfolds new revelations. The possibilities of revelation through the manifestation of the Eternal Son, are as infinite as the Son himself. As revelation does not begin with the Bible, it does not end with the Bible. Admitting that in the Bible are laid down the fundamental, spiritual, and moral principles to which every succeeding age must adjust itself, are we to deny the title and the character of revelation to the countless new phases and applications of those principles which are exhibited in the later history of mankind? Are we to limit revelation in history to the history of the Jews and of the primitive Christian Church, and to refuse to extend it to the vast and complex developments of later civilizations? Is it too much to assert that modern science furnishes a new and magnificent revelation of the Creator, or that the later history of the Christian Church, with its vast and varied record of missionary enterprise and conquest, has for us no revelations which are not to be found in the biblical account of the Jewish theocracy, and of the churches of Corinth, Ephesus, Galatia, and Colossæ?

In Scripture, as in nature, God leaves much to be filled out and formulated by the advancing knowledge and experience of mankind. The work of exegesis is

never done. "Light is sown." The successive ages reap
new harvests of light from the furrows of the Word
through the subsoil ploughing of devout criticism. Illustrations of this truth are patent to the most superficial
student. One need only compare the commentaries of
former centuries with the best of to-day, to see the advance, not only in the results, but in the methods, of exegesis. What a stride from the commentaries of Clement
and Origen, founded on the principle that all Scripture
is to be allegorically understood, or assuming a three-fold
sense of Scripture answering to body, soul, and spirit
in man; with their universal applications of isolated
phrases; with the absence of the historic sense; with
their constant assumption of an esoteric meaning; with
their mystic inferences from synonyms and repetitions;
with their admissions of apocryphal legends into New
Testament story, and their intrusion of allegorical fancies
into the simplest New Testament incidents; with their
loose and paraphrastic quotations, their different interpretations of the same passage, and their citations of
verses which have no existence—what a stride, I say, to
a monograph of De Wette, Meyer, Westcott, Lightfoot,
Godet, or Weiss, on a gospel or epistle, with its full historic background, its accurate historic perspective, its
vivid historic environment; with its minute scrutiny of
the text, its searching grammatical analysis, and its wealth
of literary, historical, geographical, and archæological
illustration! How nice the discrimination of shades of
meaning! What intimacy with the writer's modes of
thought and peculiar turns of expression! What careful
weighing of diverse interpretations! What a vigorous re-

jection of mystical and allegorical expositions! What an unflinching facing of the naked Word in its literal sense! What an unearthing of the hidden treasures of etymology and synonym! What a quick sense of idiom, as though reading a living tongue! It is like emerging from a jungle into a park. How much nearer to the original oracles has textual criticism brought us! What an advance from Erasmus, with his single mutilated manuscript of the Apocalypse, filling up the gaps in the text by translating the Vulgate into his own Greek, to the collations of the Vatican, Sinaitic, and Alexandrine codices; to chemistry and criticism joining hands for the restoration of the Codex Ephraem; to the facsimiles of Aleph and B, and to the magnificent digests of Tischendorf, Tregelles, and Westcott and Hort!

IV.—It Follows that Exegesis must be Modest and Patient.

The exegete must frankly recognize in Scripture things which he cannot explain. The Apocalypse of John, on which the interpreters of every Christian generation have exercised their ingenuity, and which has been overlaid with wagon-loads of hermeneutical nonsense, is still, much of it, a riddle; and passages emerge in almost every book of Scripture, where all that exegesis can offer is conjecture. The right attitude toward such phenomena is not that of some earlier interpreters, who insisted that an interpretation must be given at all hazards, practically assumed that *any* interpretation was better than none, and took refuge from ignorance in allegory. Rather

is the exegete to say frankly, "There is no key in the
bunch at my girdle which will fit this lock. Meanwhile
there are open doors enough. I have only to wait."
Might we not expect that the Word of which Christ is
the centre and the inspiration should sometimes say to
us, out of its very darkness, just what Christ himself said
to His disciples: "I have yet many things to say unto
you, but ye cannot bear them now?"

V.—BUT WITH ALL MODESTY AND PATIENCE, EXEGESIS MUST BE COURAGEOUS AND CANDID.

Perhaps we are never fully aware of the strength of the
preconceptions and prejudices which we bring to the
study of Scripture, until we come face to face with Scripture which flatly contradicts them, and even strikes at
what we have been wont to regard as sacred and essential.
The temptation then is either to shirk or to fight the
plain meaning of the Bible, to persist in seeking for
some explanation which will fit into our conception, and
thus to be guilty of the sin of wresting the Scriptures.
If the Bible is what we profess to believe it is, we must
trust its plain, face-meaning. We must assume that the
sacred ark needs no Uzzah's touch to steady it; that
God's truth is entirely competent to vindicate itself. We
are to march boldly up to it and to look it squarely in the
face. If it does not say what we thought it would say, or
ought to say, we are to set about correcting ourselves and
not the Bible. We are not to be scared when a correct
exegesis tells us things which startle us. When God
opens a man's eyes, he beholds *wondrous* things out of

His law.* A Calvinist has no reason for being frightened
at an Arminian text, nor an Arminian at a Calvinistic text.
The two species may be found side by side in our Lord's
own words.† It is much more likely that Calvin and
Arminius need revising and correcting than that Scripture
does. John Newton said that when he struck a Calvinistic text he was a Calvinist, and an Arminian when he
came upon an Arminian text. Calvin's principle is sound
to the very core: that it is the first business of an interpreter to let his author say what he does say, instead of
attributing to him what he thinks he ought to say.

The failure to recognize and accept these principles
has made the history of exegesis one of the most dis-
heartening and humiliating records in the history of religion. It was said by some one, of the Dutch people,
that a sufficient proof of their greatness lay in the fact
that they were above water at all; and it might, with
equal truthfulness, be said that one of the strongest evi-
dences of the divine origin and quality of the Bible is its
survival of a host of its expounders. The great distinctive fact which, along with much that is reverent, earnest,
and scholarly, marks the history of exegesis down to the
Reformation period at least, and which reasserts itself
after the glorious break made by Erasmus, Luther, and
Calvin, is the practical rejection of the *actual* Bible, and
the persistent effort to cast it into the moulds of tradition, mysticism, philosophical speculation, and ecclesias-
tical dogma. The best and most devout modern criticism
is a new protestantism, which faces the Bible as it is, and

* Psalm cxix. 18.
† For example, Matt. xi. 25-28.

places its authority above that of councils, systems, dogmas, and individual fancies. The Bible has been practically turned against itself. It has furnished ideas which
men have developed after their own fashion, and to serve
their own ends, and then have insisted that the Bible was
constructed after that fashion and for those ends. Hence
it is a familiar fact that the Bible has been cited in justi-
fication of every conceivable monstrosity of speculation,
of every refinement of cruelty, of every gross tyranny, of
every vagary of crank or fanatic, and of every distorted
moral hobby which has disfigured Christian history.
The old Latin elegiac is sadly truthful :

" Hic liber est in quo quærit sua dogmata quisque :
Invenit et pariter dogmata quisque sua." *

" Few are, perhaps, aware of the awful *extent* to which
Scripture has been distorted to evil purposes, and of the
terrible and age-long injuries which these misapplications
of Scripture by human ignorance and perversity have
inflicted upon generation after generation of unhappy
sufferers. The full record of those injuries would be the
record of ' untold agonies, and bloodshed in rivers ; ' it
would be the record of the lives of millions darkened
and blighted by intolerable superstitions ; it would be
the record of the deadliest violations of the eternal laws
of morality committed in the name of religion by those
who claimed to be its infallible defenders. . . . On
misapplications of ' Honor the king,' have been built
the ruinous opposition to national freedom ; on misap-

* This is the book in which each man seeks for his own doctrines,
and each alike finds his own.

plications of 'Thou art Peter,' the colossal usurpations of papal tyranny; on misapplications of 'Cursed be Canaan,' the shameful iniquities of the slave-trade; on misapplications of 'Compel them to come in,' the hideous crimes of the Inquisition; on misapplications of 'Thou shalt not suffer a witch to live,' the infuriated butchery of thousands of wretched women. . . . It would be the duty of one who wrote the story of Scripture interpretation to show what has been the reason why

'The devil can quote Scripture for his purpose;'

why it is that

'in religion
What damned error but some sober brow
Will bless it and approve it with a text,
Hiding the grossness with fair ornament'" *

To review this history in detail would be most interesting, but is quite impossible within my present limits. A few illustrations must suffice.

The Septuagint illustrates the remark of a modern scholar, that "even a translator has need of invincible honesty if he would avoid the misleading influences of his own *a priori* conclusions." The Septuagint, or Greek version of the Old Testament, was the popular Bible of Christ's and of Paul's time. Paul's Old Testament quotations are mostly drawn from it, as are many of the citations ascribed to Christ by the Evangelists. It was the only Bible used by the Apostolic Fathers, and was held by

* Archdeacon Farrar : " Wresting the Scriptures." Expositor. First Series, vol. xii., pp. 29, 32.

them, as by many of the later fathers, to be divinely inspired.* But the Alexandrian translators, with the enlarged range of view consequent upon their contact with Greek culture, were not proof against the temptation to modify their original Scripture, in order to evade its blows at their national pride, and to make it more agreeable and less incredible to the Gentile mind. They toned down the simple anthropomorphisms of the old Hebrew Bible, and they struck out expressions which seemed to reflect upon their leaders or to expose the moral delinquencies of their ancestors, such as the reference to Moses' "leprous" hand, and God's declaration that Israel was a "stiff-necked" people.†

Passing on to the days of Christ, we find Scripture overgrown with that enormous mass of rabbinic interpretation which, beginning as a supplement to the writ-

* For instance, Clement of Alexandria. Origen, Justin Martyr, Theodore of Mopsuestia, and Augustine. This belief rested largely upon the pseudonymous letter of Aristeas, which related that the seventy-two translators accomplished the entire translation in seventy-two days; that each translator, independently, translated the whole Old Testament, and that these translations were found, on comparison, to be verbally identical.

† Exod. iv. 6 : xxxii. 9. They inserted rabbinical legends, as that the flint knives used for circumcision in the wilderness had been buried in Joshua's grave (Josh. xxiv. 30) ; that God set bounds to the people "according to the number of the angels of God" (Deut. xxxii. 8). See also Gen. iv. 4 ; Josh. xiii. 22 ; 1 Sam. xx. 30 ; Num. xxxii. 12. The merit of the translation is very unequal. It is thought that the work of fifteen hands may be discovered. The best sections are Leviticus and Proverbs. The Prophets are often quite unintelligible. Daniel was so bad that the later version of Theodotion was substituted for it, and the original version disappeared and was believed to be no longer extant, until it was discovered at Rome in 1772.

ten law, at last superseded and threw it into contempt.
The plainest sayings of Scripture were resolved into another sense, and a rabbi declares that he that renders a
verse of Scripture as it appears, says what is not true.
Akiba assumed that the Pentateuch was a continuous
enigma, and that a meaning was to be found in every
monosyllable, and a mystic sense in every hook and
flourish of the letters. The Oral Law, subsequently
reduced to writing in the Talmud, that encyclopædia
of all the sense and nonsense of the Rabbinical Schools,
with its exaggerations, superstitions, and obscenities, its
proverbs, allegories, and legends, its romance, poetry, and
parable, completely overshadowed and superseded the
Scriptures, so that Jesus was literally justified in saying,
"Thus have ye made the commandment of God *of none
effect* through your tradition."

In the succeeding period of exegesis, that of the Alexandrian Schools, we see indeed the culmination of Greek
influence upon Jewish thought, but we also see the mis-
chief of the rabbinical interpretation perpetuated and
active in that distinctive feature of Alexandrian exegesis
—the allegorical method, which, in turn, has transmitted
its influence down to a very late period. Allegorical interpretation is not born of *biblical* exegesis. The Brah-
mins employed it upon the Vedas, the Sufis upon the
Koran, and the Stoics upon Homer. It grew out of the
desire to find a point of junction for an old faith with a
new, wider, and more philosophic culture. It was the
medium of a compromise between loyalty to tradition and
the requirement of a broader intellectual outlook. It was
an attempt to extract the new ideas from the old writings.

The Alexandrian Jew undertook to harmonize the
severe dogmas of the old Hebrew faith with the Hellenic
philosophy, and to find the teachings of Zeno and of Plato
in Moses and the prophets. The only possible instru-
ment of this process was allegory, which found its high
priest in Philo. Under his treatment the Law of Moses
and the histories of Scripture became wellnigh unrecog-
nizable. The fundamental thought of his great commentary on Genesis is, that the history of mankind as related
in that book is nothing else than a system of psychology
and ethics, the different individuals who figure in the
history denoting different states of the soul. Abraham is
the type of a Stoic seeking truth. Attaining the knowledge of God, he marries Sarah, who is abstract wisdom.
Jacob, arriving at Bethel at sunset, is human wisdom
coming to the divine Word, where the perceptive faculty
is found to be useless. Moses is intelligence; Aaron,
speech; Enoch, repentance; Esau, rude disobedience;
Rachel, innocence. "The most external occurrences of
scriptural history," to quote the words of Schürer, become in his hands mines of instruction concerning the
supreme problems of human existence." The Bible is
converted into a philosophical romance.

Nor do the operation and the influence of this vicious
method cease with the Alexandrian School. They appear
in full and baneful vigor in the exegesis of the Fathers.
The sincere and beautiful piety of Clement of Rome; the
catholicity, candor, and simplicity of Justin Martyr; the
learning of Irenæus; the intellectual vigor of Tertullian;
the culture of Clement of Alexandria; the homiletic and
expository skill of Origen—none of these avail to pre-

serve their exegesis from the taint of the rabbis and of
Philo. They alter, they misquote, they introduce Jewish
legends, they appeal to apocryphal writings as inspired,
they resolve the plainest statements and narratives into
allegory, they proclaim the words of the Septuagint to be
the very words of the Holy Spirit, even when they differ
most widely from the original Hebrew. In Clement and
Origen, notwithstanding their larger learning and broader
culture, the influence of Philo is apparent in their attempt to reconcile the Bible and Greek philosophy, and
to vindicate a Christian *gnosis* which penetrates to a hidden, oracular, mystical sense of Scripture. On such a
basis allegory runs rampant. With all Origen's depth of
thought, grammatical knowledge, expository skill, and
earnest piety, he is dominated by the theory of verbal
dictation in its most pronounced form, and by the assumption that the Bible is throughout homogeneous and,
in every particular, supernaturally perfect. From the
plain contradictions of Scripture to this position, the only
refuge is allegory, and the doctrine of the threefold sense,
literal, moral, and mystical. As the anthropomorphisms
of the Old Testament could not be literally true; as such
stories as the drunkenness of Noah and the incest of Lot
were immoral; as some of the Old Testament precepts
were manifestly unjust—these must all be interpreted in
a mystical sense. The water-pots at Cana, containing
two or three firkins apiece, mean the Scriptures, which
were intended to purify the Jews, and which sometimes
contain two firkins—the moral and literal senses—and
sometimes three, the spiritual sense also. The six
water-pots indicate that the world was created in six

days. The ass on which Jesus rode into Jerusalem represents the letter of the Old Testament, and the ass' foal, which was gentle and submissive, the New Testament, and the two apostles who go to loose them are the moral and mystical senses.

Notwithstanding the hints of a sounder criticism and of a better method in Dionysius of Alexandria, in the school of Antioch represented by Theodore of Mopsuestia and Chrysostom, and later still in Jerome, the exegetic pendulum takes a backward swing in Augustine, far greater as a theologian and dialectician than as an exegete. He was ignorant of Hebrew and but poorly equipped in Greek. In him the Rabbinic and Philonian method, and the superstitious reverence for the Septuagint survive, and in him appears that widely-spread and most mischievous error of interpreting Scripture in accordance with dogmatic prepossessions, formulated in his rule that the Bible must be interpreted according to Church orthodoxy,* and expressed still more forcibly in his criticism of the Letter of Mani : "I would not believe the gospel if I were not moved thereto by the authority of the Catholic Church." The victory remained for the time with the allegorists. The Western theologians crushed Theodore of Mopsuestia, and the school of Antioch was anathematized.

It is not my purpose to give even an outline of the history of exegesis. I shall not therefore detain you amid the dreariness of the period from the seventh to the twelfth century, when the Papacy had established its des-

* Scriptura non asserit nisi fidem catholicum.—De Doctr. Christ., iii. 10.

potism over the minds of men ; when the church backed
with penal thunders her claim to be the sole, infallible
interpreter of Scripture, and treated the study of its
original tongues as little better than a crime. It is a re-
lief to escape from the sombre shadow of that eclipse of
learning ; from the huge piles of dogmatic tomes ; from
the uncritical, second-hand, hap-hazard patristic compi-
lations of Bede and Alcuin ; from the interlinear and
marginal glosses of Strabo and Anselm of Laon, and from
the grammatical and mystical platitudes of Hugo of St.
Victor. Nor can I dwell upon the scholastic era, when the
Bible served as the handmaid of Aristotle ; nor upon the
great exegetic revival under the auspices of Erasmus,
Luther, and Calvin, a prince among exegetes ; nor upon
the sad relapse of the post-Reformation era, with its new
scholasticism built upon party-creeds, and fettering and
emasculating exegesis by an arbitrary and dictatorial con-
fessionalism.

In the brief time which remains, I can only summarize
a few of the results of a false exegesis which the past has
transmitted to later times, and against which the best
biblical scholarship of this age is arrayed.

First of all is the identification of inspiration with me-
chanical, literal, verbal infallibility, a doctrine embodied
in the seventeenth century formulas that the writers of
Scriptures are "amanuenses of God," "hands of Christ,"
"scribes and notaries of the Holy Spirit," "living and
writing pens." The extent to which this was pressed is
well-nigh incredible. The Hellenic Consensus of 1675,
drawn up by Turretin and Heidegger, asserted that the
very vowel-points and accents of the Hebrew Bible were

divinely inspired. It was even discussed whether the vowel-points originated with Adam, Moses, or Ezra : the actual fact being that they originated with the Masorites, about the sixth century of the Christian era. The Wittemberg faculty, in 1638, decreed that to speak of barbarisms or solecisms in the New Testament Greek was blasphemy against the Holy Ghost ; and the Purists of the seventeenth century maintained that to deny that God gave the New Testament in anything else than pure, classical Greek, was to imperil the doctrine of inspiration.

Such absurdities have, happily, become obsolete, though their underlying principle still crops out in the modern Church. The doctrine of verbal inerrancy is in plain contradiction of the actual phenomena of Scripture. It necessitates as its corollary inerrant transmission and inerrant interpretation. It is based wholly upon an *a priori* assumption of what inspiration *must be*, and not upon the Bible as it actually exists ; it is contrary to the analogy of God's procedure in other departments of His administration ; it has no warrant in the teachings of the early Church, and it renders a true exegesis simply impossible.*

* It is difficult to avoid severe expressions concerning the attempts of certain divines, and writers in the religious journals, to stigmatize as unorthodox those who deny the verbal infallibility of Scripture, and to represent them as drawing their arguments from sceptical sources. The question of Christian courtesy, charity, and candor entirely apart, such utterances betray an ignorance which is unpardonable in men who assume to shape and direct public opinion. It ought not to be necessary to inform such that the denial of verbal infallibility is not only no new thing, but that it has been asserted by a host of Christian scholars, of the first rank, since the days of Jerome, not to go

Next follows the principle of allegorical interpretation,
which asserts itself with more or less power throughout
the entire history of exegesis from the Rabbinical to the
post-Reformation era, and which at once sweeps away
all fixed standards of interpretation, and puts the reader
at the mercy of each expositor's individual fancy. On its
mischievousness in ignoring the element of growth in
biblical history and reducing it to a dead level, I have not
time to dwell. The allegorical *application* of Scripture,
within reasonable limits, is, indeed, legitimate ; but that
is quite another and a different matter from allegorical
interpretation. The evil of this method appears in a certain class of popular expositions, the atrocities of which
would fill volumes, in which the preacher rides, Jehu-like,
across country, some rampant fancy of his own, instead of
following soberly and reverently in the track of the Word.
There is, unfortunately, too much truth in the severe re-

farther back. Among these may be named Luther and Calvin ; Rich-
ard Baxter and Samuel Rutherford ; Hooker, Chillingworth, Tillot-
son, Doddridge, Warburton, Paley, Lowth ; Archbishop Whately,
Bishops Thirlwall and Heber, Dean Alford, Bishops Lightfoot and
Westcott, Archdeacon Farrar and Professor Sanday. The Church of
Rome has never fully decreed the doctrine. It was denied by Car-
dinal Newman ; and the Bishop of Amycla, assistant to the Archbishop of Westminster, asserts that " Catholics are under no sort or
obligation to believe that inspiration extends to the words of Holy
Scripture as well as to the subject-matter which is therein contained."
Among the Germans may be mentioned the revered names of Tho-
luck and Neander, with Meyer, Stier, Lange, and Dorner. Many oth-
ers might be added to the list. The doctrine is nowhere stated in the
Westminster Standards. Their authors were content to assert the
fact of inspiration without defining its mode and degrees. The same
is true of the Anglican Articles.

mark of a living scholar, that "homiletics have been, to
an incredible extent, the *Phylloxera vastatrix* of exegesis,
and that preachers have become privileged misinterpret-
ers." That the commentary, even down to a late period,
has not escaped this nuisance, may be seen from Bishop
Wordsworth's comment on the story of Jael and Sisera,
where we are told that there is a parallel between the
tent-peg with which Jael shattered Sisera's skull, and
the stake by which the Gentiles enlarge the church; that
there is a comparison of the tent-peg with the cross; and
that there is also a parallel between Jael and the Virgin
Mary.

Thirdly comes the exaggeration of the so-called "analogy of faith," a favorite phrase with the Reformers, and
originally signifying that Scripture should be explained
in accordance with Scripture. The phrase itself was
based on a mistranslation of Romans xii. 6 ; * and while
it imposed a salutary check upon the practice of isolating
passages of Scripture, and carried the sound principle
that individual passages should be interpreted according
to the general tenor of Scripture, it soon passed, practically, into the rule that interpretation must conform to
correct dogma. Thus, as has been said, "it paved the
way for the distortions and sophistries of the later Prot-
estant scholasticism, and turned the Old Testament especially into a sort of obscure forest, in which dogma and
allegory hunt in couples to catch what they can." †

The abuse of the principle links itself with the allegor-

---

* κατὰ τὴν ἀναλογίαν τῆς πίστεως, "according to the *proportion* of
faith."

† F. W. Farrar : Bampton Lectures for 1885.

ical method, and with the want of the historic sense in interpretation. It exaggerates the homogeneousness of Scripture by making every part in every age have direct and designed reference to every other part. It thus ignores historical perspective, and makes the Bible like an Egyptian mural painting, which is all foreground.

To strike at the abuse is not to surrender the unity of Scripture. We may, for instance, firmly hold by the fact of Messianic prophecy in the Old Testament, without, as was said of Justin Martyr, applying all the sticks and pieces of wood in the Old Testament to the cross; without, like Clement of Rome, construing Rahab's scarlet cord into a prophecy of redemption by blood; without, as Barnabas, making the "tree planted by rivers of water" mean the cross and baptism. While the Bible, as a whole, turns on Christ, it is even possible to abuse Luther's rule, that Christ is to be found everywhere in Scripture. Solomon's Song does not signify the love of Christ for His Church : yet this exploded allegorical interpretation underlies its citation in the "Westminster Confession," where passages from it are used as prooftexts of the doctrine of "effectual calling," and of the statement that true believers may have the assurance of their salvation shaken by God's withdrawing the light of His countenance.* And, while I am speaking of the "Confession," let me say that the revision of its prooftexts, already inaugurated, should go much deeper than the insertion or omission of a text here and there. The present system of proof-texts is framed according to the principles of interpretation current in 1647 ; and these

---

* Chap. x. sect. 1 ; chap. xviii. sect. 4.

principles, and not merely the individual texts, should be examined and dealt with. When, as we have seen, "effectual calling " is argued from a false, allegorical interpretation of a passage in Canticles; when the "the wages of sin is death," and, "for every idle word that men shall speak, they shall give account," are cited in support of the statement that "no sin is so small but it deserves damnation ;"* when the statement that all the books of the Old and New Testaments "are given by inspiration of God to be the rule of faith and life," appeals to Revelation xxii. 18, 19, "If any man shall add unto these things, God shall add unto him the plagues that are written in this book," etc.;† when the statement that the Hebrew and Greek originals of the Bible have been "kept pure in all ages " is backed by " Till heaven and earth pass, one jot or one tittle shall in no wise pass from the law, till all be fulfilled ; "‡ when it is deduced from "The foundation of God standeth sure, having this seal, the Lord knoweth them that are His," that the number of the elect and of the reprobate is definitely and unchangeably fixed by the divine decree,§ it is quite time that revision should go down to the basis of interpretation.

Lastly, the subordination of exegesis to dogma, the baneful inheritance from Augustine, and from the post-Reformation era. Here devout criticism, scholarly intelligence, and the whole energy of the freedom with which Christ makes free must be concentrated in order to preserve the liberty of the individual Christian and the rightful supremacy of Scripture. I do not undervalue

* Chap. xv. sect. 4. † Chap. i. sect. 2.
‡ Chap. i. sect. 8. § Chap. iii. sect. 4.

creeds, confessions, and theologies. They have their
place and their work, and both are important ; but the
time has fully come for the roundest and most practical
assertion that the Scriptures are the ONLY infallible rule
of faith and practice—the Scriptures as read with the
Holy Spirit's guidance and light, and interpreted according to the canons of a reverent and scholarly exegesis :
that no theological dogma is binding upon the Christian
conscience, which is not based upon a fair and sound interpretation of Scripture as it stands. The time is past
for the Church to be held to the horrible and unscriptur-
al doctrine of a divine predestination of a portion of mankind to everlasting damnation, by the words " Jacob
have I loved and Esau have I hated," and by the ninth,
tenth, and eleventh chapters of Romans, which have no
more to do with divine predestination to eternal life or
death than the Iliad of Homer or the Clouds of Aris-
tophanes.

Union Seminary holds by the Bible. It exalts its authority ; it accepts that authority as supreme ; it uncom-
promisingly accepts the Bible as the only infallible rule
of faith and practice ; as the only legitimate basis of
gospel preaching ; as containing the only and sufficient
revelation of Him whose name is above every name—the
only Redeemer of mankind, the Head of the Church.
Its faculty and its directors alike stake their salvation
on its truth. Why will the Church not see that its
teachers are the friends and the champions of the Bible,
and not its carping critics ? That it is because of their
love and reverence for it, because they see, better than
the general religious public, the subtlety, power, and in-

tellectual acuteness of the attacks aimed at it, that they
are trying to save it from the wounds of its friends, from
modes of defence which only expose it to deadlier
thrusts; trying to let the divine inspiration which is in
it vindicate its own power and majesty; trying to put its
interpretation upon a basis which will successfully resist
the shocks of a godless rationalism?

It shall be, as it ever has been, the delight and the
pride of Union Seminary to magnify the Bible before the
eyes of men, and to assert its principles and its personal,
divine centre, Jesus Christ, as the solution of all the great
world problems, the mould and the inspiration of perfect
character, the basis of a perfect society.

It recognizes the need of the Holy Spirit's aid and light
in the study of the Word. It has no sympathy with a
cold and purely intellectual and scholastic criticism.
But it will continue to stand, as it has stood from the
first, for the largest liberty of interpretation; for the
claim of scholarly exegesis to a respectful hearing; for
the right to limit to matters of faith and duty its subscrip-
tion to the doctrine of the infallibility and authority of
Scripture; for a square, brave facing of the plain meaning of Scripture; for the ascertainment and establishment
of the objective historical sense of the Bible as against
mere subjective speculations; for the Bible first, and confessions after the Bible.

In the eloquent words of the beloved and lamented
Meyer: "It is just when exegetical research is perfectly
unprejudiced, impartial, and free—and thus all the more
consciously and consistently guided simply and solely by
those historically-given factors of its science—that it is

able with genuine humility to render to the Church, so far as the latter maintains its palladium in the pure word of God, real and wholesome service for the present and the future. However deep may be the heavings of conflicting elements within it, and however long may be the duration of the painful throes which shall at last issue in a happier time for the Church, when men's minds shall have attained a higher union, the pure word of Scripture, in its historical truth and clearness, and in its world-subduing, divine might, disengaged from every addition of human scholasticism and its dividing formulæ, must and shall at length become once more a wonderful power of peace unto unity of faith and love." *

* Introduction to the Commentary on Romans.